W9-CFK-014

Cat'n Around

Written by **Gabriella Klein**

Photography by **Brad Jaeck** and **Carol Hansen**

Cat'n Around Downtown

Racine, Wisconsin

Shown on the front cover are the felines that received top prizes in the Cat'n Around Downtown competition. Left to right are Catfish, created by Denise Roberts McKee, first place; Cleocatra, created by Janet Mrazek, David Gaura and Linda Morafcik, second place; and Cat Fishing in Winter, created by Bill Reid, third place. All are profiled elsewhere in this book.

Special thanks to The Journal Times for the Fourth Fest 2002 photo by Ron Kuentsler on page 17.

ISBN 0-9741541-0-5

Photographs and text
© 2003 Downtown Racine Corporation, Inc.

Graphic design by
Design Partners, Inc., Racine, Wisconsin

This book may not be reproduced in whole or in part by any means (with the exception of short quotes for the purpose of review) without the permission of Downtown Racine Corporation, Inc.

Created, designed and printed in the United States.

Collaborating with Cats

"I am the cat that walks by himself and all places are alike to me." So wrote Rudyard Kipling in one of his *Just So Stories*.

In Downtown Racine, the creative kitties decorating Main and Sixth streets this summer are anything but loners. They – and all who worked on this public art event and were involved with this book – are collaborators in the fullest sense.

Cat'n Around Downtown, the second annual public art event sponsored jointly by Downtown Racine Corporation and *The Journal Times*, and this book about the cats show what happens with collaboration.

Last year's book, *Dog Days of Summer*, captured the special time of Downtown Racine's first public art event. We feel this year's book, *Cat'n Around*, shows that fantastic felines are as much fun as creative canines.

We'd like to thank the Downtown Racine Corporation staff, led by Executive Director Kathy Hansen, for all their hard work on Cat'n Around Downtown and for their help with this book.

As with Dog Days of Summer, Gene Johnson was pivotal in bringing the cats to Downtown Racine. Her commitment is key to the success of this collaboration. Our thanks to this year's artists. They gave their utmost –

really beyond imagination – as you'll see in this book and when you tour Main and Sixth streets in Downtown Racine. Thanks also to their sponsors, without whom Cat'n Around Downtown would not have been possible.

The creative staff at Downtown Racine's Design Partners, Inc., truly collaborated on the look of this book. We thank them for their creative talents and for their willingness to work so hard on this project.

My sincere thanks to our excellent photographers, Brad Jaeck and Carol Hansen. Working with them on last year's *Dog Days of Summer* book was fun, and I must admit we had even more fun with this year's book.

Every writer needs a good proofreader. I'm fortunate in that I had two: Terry Leopold of Downtown Racine Corporation and my husband Don. They have proofing eyes that are beyond belief.

I also thank Terry for putting up with my frequent voice mails, e-mails and telephone calls. And I thank Don for his patience and for keeping our household together while I was having fun with this book.

Collaborating with cats? You bet! We've not walked by ourselves but together, for what we know is a wonderful Cat'n Around Downtown experience in Racine in 2003.

– *Gabriella Klein*

Table of Contents

Cat'n Around Downtown

Racine, Wisconsin

Cat'n Around Downtown

Cats, cats and more cats – 151 of them in all. Contrary to the belief that cats cannot be herded, these all are.

These creative felines are Cat'n Around Downtown from May 6 to September 22 this year, in the second annual public art event sponsored by Downtown Racine Corporation and *The Journal Times*.

"In 2002 we had Dog Days of Summer," explained Kathy Hansen, executive director of Downtown Racine Corporation. "So it's totally logical that cats have equal time this year."

This year's Downtown public art event includes cats in a wide array of adornment. Some are fashion plates. Others conjure up history. Some change from being cats to being other critters, like caterpillars, owls and even a dog. Some take on the nautical nature of Downtown Racine. Some show the importance of food in their lives. Others even dare to represent the world of work. The creativity of the artists is plainly evident when one studies these amazing cats and what they have become.

Where Did The Cats Come From?

Plans to have cats in 2003 started late last summer, while the 149 pooches of Dog Days of Summer were still enjoying their fame on the 10-block Downtown stretch on Main and Sixth streets.

When Downtown Racine Corporation's committee determined it would have cats for its 2003 public art event, it turned to the experts – those who had created the molds for Dog Days of Summer.

The firm, Cowpainters LLC of Chicago, came into being in 1999, after its owner, Nancy Albrecht, had created *Chi-cow-go* for Chicago's 1999 Cows on Parade. She was asked to develop table-top versions of cows as private commissions, and Cowpainters was born.

Jessica Danowski hugs Polka Dot Cat as cats are delivered April 16.

Michael and Vernay Mueller of Racine and their daughter, Tina Parise-Mitchell of West Bend, deliver their completed cats to Historic Century Market.

Terry Leopold, left, and Jean Garbo, both members of the Downtown Racine Corporation staff, check in Kitty City, created by Kelly Smith.

Crowds throng around the dogs at the auction October 13. The event raised $146,000 in net proceeds divided between Downtown Racine Corporation and the new Racine Art Museum.

Gene Johnson of Racine, the driving force behind both Dog Days of Summer and Cat'n Around Downtown, worked with Cowpainters to develop just the right cat. She determined Downtown Racine would have cats in two positions – standing and sitting. Johnson worked with Albrecht and Cowpainters' operations manager and artist Kirsten Graf, who explained, "These cats were created for the Downtown Racine project. I have a cat so that was a place to start. Then I wanted surfaces that were 'beefy,' so the artists would have something to work with."

Because each cat is created individually, sizes and weights vary among the 151. The standing cats measure 28 inches from the ground to the tops of their heads and 33 inches to the tops of their tails, 29 inches front to back, with bodies about 10 inches wide. They weigh about 25 pounds each. The sitting cats are 28 inches top to bottom, 18 inches front to back and 14 inches wide. They weigh in at about 20 pounds each. The Downtown Racine project has 51 sitting cats and 100 who are standing.

"We're excited to be part of Downtown Racine's public art project again this year," Albrecht said. "Your community is a great place and we really enjoy working with Mrs. Johnson and all the Racinians involved with Cat'n Around Downtown."

The cat figures, unadorned, made their first public appearance October 13, 2002, during the Dog Days of Summer public auction. More than 1,200 people flocked to the under-the-tent event, at which the 149 dogs raised $146,000 in net proceeds, which were divided between Downtown Racine Corporation and Racine Art Museum.

Billboards and other attention grabbers help build excitement for the start of the cats' public display May 6.

Kathy Hansen, Downtown Racine Corporation executive director, unveils the two cats during the Dog Days of Summer auction October 13, 2002.

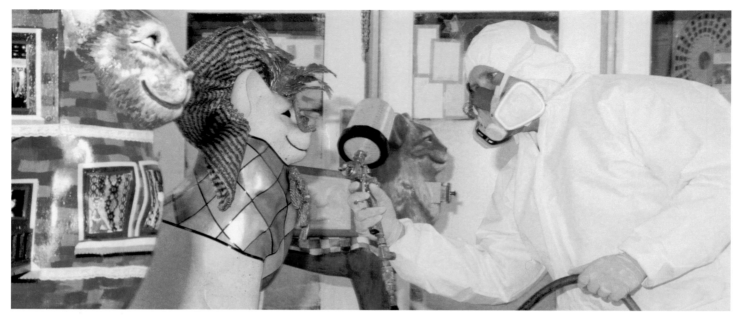

Joseph Machalik of Uptown Auto Body clear-coats A Cat's House while Mardi Gras Meow and Kitchen Kitty wait their turns. Several Racine auto body shops, including Uptown, A-1 and Racine Auto Body, clear-coated the cats free of charge in support of this year's Downtown Racine public art event.

Call for Artist Proposals

Cat'n Around Downtown picked up speed in December, when the call for artist proposals went out. By the time the entry deadline arrived January 15, more than 400 ideas for creative cats had been submitted.

A six-member panel had its work cut out for it. Starting January 21, it reviewed each and every design proposal. Criteria for acceptance included originality, creativity, feasibility, durability to withstand not only more than five months on public display but also lifetime permanence. Decisions were difficult to make, even with using a point system. The panel spent many hours during several days in this selection process.

The Artists Get to Work

By the end of January, artists were notified. They picked up the cats they would turn into creative masterpieces. They had until April 16 to complete their work and deliver their creations. By the time the feline artworks were finished, more than 200 people had been somehow involved in their creation.

Simultaneously, sponsors indicated which cats they wanted to sponsor. This year's sponsor list, found in the index on page 120, includes 142 businesses, organizations and individuals. Sponsorship cost was $350, with $100 going to the artist for supplies and $250 paying for the cost of the cat sculpture.

From April 16 until May 6, when they hit the streets, the cats needed a place to stay. Their temporary home, and

headquarters for other Cat'n Around Downtown activities, was Historic Century Market at 522 Sixth Street, owned by Jim Spodick.

Cats on Display

The completed cats made their collective media appearance at a press conference May 1, and their first public appearance May 3 during *Jammin' with the Cool Cats*, the annual fund-raiser sponsored by Downtown Racine Corporation.

As of May 6, these creative kitties are spending their summer Cat'n Around Downtown. About 80 are mounted on platforms and spend their days outdoors and nights inside. The remainder are found in windows of businesses on both Main and Sixth streets.

The felines go to their permanent homes October 4 when they are sold at auction. Proceeds from the auction are shared by Downtown Racine Corporation and Racine Heritage Museum, which plans to open a new facility in Downtown Racine in 2005.

Amy Davis, creator of Pic"Cat"so, is flanked by daughters Rachel (back) and Lydia, as they admire other feline creations delivered on April 16.

Downtown Racine
...an exciting destination

Fesitval Hall (green roofed building in center), completed in late 1987 on the shore of Lake Michigan, was one of the first new structures in Downtown Racine's renaissance. Racine Art Museum (left) opened this May and the Johnson Building (right) was completed in May 2002.

Main and Sixth is a key intersection in Downtown Racine.

Sixth Street is becoming well-known as Racine's Heart of Arts, with its theater, art galleries and unique shops.

There was a time, really not that many years ago, that Downtown Racine was a place to pass through on one's way to somewhere else. It was not considered much of a stopping-off point.

All that has changed – dramatically.

Today, Downtown Racine definitely is an exciting destination in its own right. People come Downtown to enjoy the many amenities it has to offer, from excellent shopping and dining, to entertainment, Lake Michigan and Root River action, museums, and just plain fun. People once again live Downtown, in the many revitalized historic buildings and new condominiums and townhouses.

A Bit of History

Downtown Racine is right on the shore of Lake Michigan, where the Root River meets the lake. It is about 30 miles south of Milwaukee and 80 miles north of Chicago.

This was where the city was founded in 1848 and from there it grew into a major industrial and residential complex, with Downtown providing the central mercantile and social point. The city prospered and grew.

All that changed in the 1960s, as Racine experienced what other downtown areas, especially those in the industrialized Midwest, endured – the flight outward. Downtown Racine found itself beset with empty storefronts, decaying buildings, and general lack of interest in its welfare. Except for the dedicated fishermen, no one much cared about either the lake or the river.

In the 1970s, area business people and residents took a closer look and knew that Downtown Racine could return to its earlier glory days. They went to work.

The process was not an easy one. It had some excellent starts – and then stops. But by the late 1990s it was clear Downtown Racine was on its way to becoming a thriving Southeastern Wisconsin community center. Today, it is just that – and much more.

The Lakefront Artist Fair draws huge crowds to Downtown Racine's Festival Park every May.

13

Downtown Racine Today

Downtown Racine is fast becoming the vibrant center of this community of more than 81,000 people. Many factors have contributed to that new vibrancy. Among them is the Downtown Racine Corporation plan for the area, bordered by the Root River on the north, Lake Michigan on the east, Eighth Street on the south and Center Street on the west. This plan was the first one to have had input from the community and it was ultimately adopted by the Racine City Council as the land use plan for Downtown.

Left: Dining establishments of all kinds – from the quick and casual to the more formal – are plentiful in Downtown Racine.

Below: Splash Square in the Sam Johnson Parkway is the ideal place to cool off during hot summer days and early evenings.

Heather Jirgensen of Racine enjoys a moment of tranquility on the walkway surrounding Reefpoint Marina.

Devoted on-shore fishermen enjoy the sport on Lake Michigan, Downtown Racine's eastern border.

The Sam Johnson Parkway, on Main and Sixth streets, is a great gathering spot from which to enjoy Downtown Racine's view of Lake Michigan.

The principles of the Downtown plan include the following:
• Utilize special Downtown natural resource features.
• Preserve historic architectural environment of the Downtown.
• Utilize existing assets.
• Develop a pedestrian-friendly Downtown.
• Increase residential development.
• Promote business development.
• Increase office development.
• Identify catalyst projects.
• Develop community consensus.
• Meet and exceed established goals and expectations.

Balloon artist Tim Glander prepares a creation for Cori Porasik of Racine.

Jessica Hunter often enjoys shopping on Main Street with her grandmother, Sue Meredith. During a recent trip, Jessica met Maggie, one of several dogs who "works" in Downtown stores.

Racine's annual Fourth Fest parade draws crowds of up to 100,000 to Downtown Racine each July 4. In 2002, Copper and Patriot were honorary parade marshals. They're shown with their creators, Patriot's Nancy Tyyska (left) and Copper's Stephanie Andersen.

Among Downtown's major new-construction achievements are One Main Centre, located at State and Main streets near the Root River, and the Johnson Building, opened in May 2002 at 555 Main Street.

New Museums

Two new museums are helping reinforce Downtown Racine as a destination.

The Racine Art Museum, located on the northeast corner of Main and Fifth streets, opened this May and houses one of North America's most significant collections of contemporary craft. Its collection focuses on work from internationally recognized artists in ceramics, fibers, glass, metals and wood.

The museum's gift store opened last November, in time for the holiday shopping season.

This exciting new facility was the beneficiary of half the net proceeds raised at 2002's Dog Days of Summer auction.

Top: The Farmer's Market, in operation from May through October, is a popular place for vendors and customers alike every Saturday morning.

Left: Jimmy Poplawski (standing), Nicholas Davidovic (seated left) and Marquis Smith, all of Racine, find the steps at Monument Square the ideal place to relax for a few minutes.

"Explore – discover – innovate" is the theme for the new Racine Heritage Museum, scheduled to open in Downtown Racine in 2005. It will replace the current museum at Seventh and Main streets.

This new facility will be situated at the corner of Sixth Street and Library Drive, just west of Lake Michigan and south of Festival Hall.

Half the net proceeds from the Cat'n Around Downtown cat auction October 4 will go to the Racine Heritage Museum.

Top: The conceptual rendering of the new Racine Heritage Museum shows that it will become a signature building for Downtown Racine.

Right: Jerry Cross, Reva Holmes and Jayne Steffans (left to right) enjoy shopping at Artists Gallery, the artists' co-op venture on Sixth Street.

The Root River, which flows into Lake Michigan, forms Downtown Racine's northern border.

Amazing Architecture

These seven cats lend their bodies to all things architectural – from doors to entire buildings. You'll even note a couple of "different" kinds of houses.

"Cats are successful underachievers...
What other creature can lay around the house doing nothing beyond purring, and still get free food and T L C?"

Jim Aites

21

A Cat's House

"Styled after the building on Third and Main; cat people live in an apartment with a sense of fun and playfulness."

Artist: Marcia Sykes, Racine

Marcia Sykes holds a bachelor of arts degree from University of Wisconsin-Parkside and a master's degree from National Louis University. She currently teaches at Washington Park High School in Racine. She also enjoys taking classes at Pigeon Lake in the summer.

Sponsor: Re/Max Southeast, Inc.

Ar-cat-ecture

"Based on Frank Lloyd Wright's architectural structure and graphics."

Artist: Julia Fawcett, Racine

Julia Fawcett is a senior at Horlick High School. She will be furthering her education in the arts and wishes to pursue a career as an artist. She hopes to attend the Illinois Institute of Art in Chicago. Her hobbies include playing the piano and drums, and she also works part-time as a model.

Sponsor: Bluelines, Inc.

Cat House

"Waiting in the doorway of the cat house…"

**Artists: Studio 261 – Dale Caron,
Laurence Faujour, Maria Greer,
Alice Hazarian, Judie Kaprelian,
Lyle Peters, Catherine Sauvage,
Dawn Sutherland, Racine**

Eight artists, all part of Studio 261, located in the Von Schroeder Building on 16th Street in Racine, have banded together to create this cat. As painters, they work with oil paints, watercolors and pastels and have participated in many local and area exhibits. Their work may be seen at the Artists Gallery on Sixth Street or by appointment at Studio 261. Several are current or former students of Joan Parsons at Charles A. Wustum Museum of Fine Arts.

Sponsor: N. Christensen and Son Real Estate, Inc.

Hide and Seek

"The Wind Point lighthouse – a cat seeks out hiding animals; a lighthouse seeks out boats in the night."

Artist: Kathleen Lippold, Racine

A teacher in Racine Unified schools for more than 20 years, Kathleen Lippold works with special education students at the elementary level. She's always enjoyed art and considers it a challenge to create and work with many different kinds of media. She watercolor paints, mainly scenic buildings and lighthouses, as a hobby.

Sponsor: Dr. Richard M. Wagner Oral and Maxillo/Facial Surgery.

Housecat

"Made into a house, if possible achieved with real building materials."

Artist: Jason Paul Johannes, Oregon, Wisconsin

A native of Howards Grove, Wisconsin, Jason Paul Johannes had a strong interest in art from childhood. Following a move to Oregon as a teen, he graduated with a bachelor of arts degree from Lawrence University in Appleton, with a major in mathematics and computer science and a minor in art. He presently works in information technology at Space-Metrics, LLC in Oregon.

Sponsor: The LaFleur Family

Josephine

"A replica of some of the doors in my home."

Artist: Rachel Ballantyne, Racine

Rachel Ballantyne currently owns a home designed by Racine architect John Randal McDonald. Her cat's design is based on the original "JRM" doors found throughout her home, and her cat is named after McDonald's wife. Ballantyne and her husband Tad coordinate many functions with McDonald and more than 50 of his Wisconsin homeowners, including lecture requests and home tours.

Sponsor: John Randal McDonald

The Cat House

"Focuses on the story of the Moulin Rouge as a supporter of the arts and theatre, and a love story."

Artist: K8 Prange, Milwaukee

An art director at Jacobson Rost, Sheboygan, K8 Prange graduated from the University of Wisconsin-Milwaukee with a bachelor of fine arts degree, and the Milwaukee Institute of Art and Design. A native of Sheboygan, she enjoys working with mixed media, juxtaposing still images and photography to form collages. Her favorite freetime activities include freelance design, studying film techniques and theater.

Sponsor: Design Partners, Inc.

Aquatic Adventures

*I*t's a well-known fact that cats and water are not natural mixers. Yet these 14 artistic creations seem to have defied that fact.

"Cats are intended to teach us that not everything in nature has a purpose."

Garrison Keillor

Acat

"Dreaming about Lake Michigan ferry service between Wisconsin and Michigan."

Artist: Bruce Renquist, Racine

Bruce Renquist is an industrial designer. He is a graduate of the Layton School of Art, Milwaukee, and was chairman of Renquist Associates of Racine for 32 years. He helped found and was chairman of the board of trustees of the Milwaukee Institute of Art and Design.

Sponsor: Dover Flag and Map

Belle's Root River Holiday

"Belle spends her day fishing in the Root River."

Artist: Linda M. Silvasi-Kelly, Baileys Harbor, Wisconsin

A Racine native who took childhood classes at Wustum Museum of Fine Arts, Linda Silvasi-Kelly has her bachelor of fine arts degree from the University of Wisconsin-Green Bay. A freelance artist, she works in several media. She has illustrated several books and designed ads, logos and brochures. She also does faux painting, trompe l'oeil, stenciling, and hand-paints furniture and walls.

Sponsor: Harbor Lite Yacht Club

Bob Cat

"Serving as the bobber to catch fish."

Artist: **Don Bugalecki, Kenosha**

Don Bugalecki is a senior graphic designer at SC Johnson, where he has been employed for 30 years. A graduate of Layton School of Art and Design, he has designed at least 20 of the crowd-pleasing Johnson floats that have appeared in Racine's Fourth Fest parades. He enjoys working with water colors and also restoring antique cars.

Sponsor: **Johnson Outdoors Inc.**

Cat Fishing in Winter

"Taking advantage of this winter sport."

Artist: **Bill Reid, Racine**

Nationally known sculptor Bill Reid received his bachelor of fine arts degree from Kansas City (Missouri) Art Institute and his master's degree in fine arts from Cranbook Academy of Art in Bloomfield Hills, Michigan. He also received certification in pressure vessel welding at the Tulsa Welding School in Oklahoma.

Sponsor: **Schorsch Management/ Green Bay Meadows Apartments**

Catfish

"Smooth glass and color tile give this mosaic cat its 'fishy' exterior."

Artist: Denise Roberts McKee, Racine

Denise Roberts McKee is chief operating officer and partner of Stunt Puppy Entertainment, Inc., a software development company specializing in children's and family entertainment. She oversees operations for the firm's offices in Racine and Foster City, California. She holds a bachelor of science degree in art from the University of Wisconsin-Madison. Her free-time projects center on creating mosaic pieces from tile, metal and found objects.

Sponsor: Stunt Puppy Entertainment, Inc.

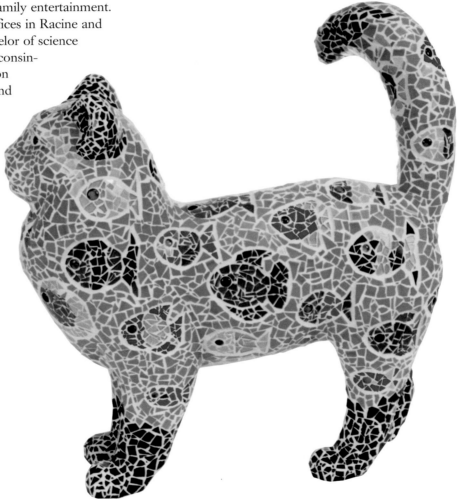

Cat-"tails"

"Scenes from a pond; wildlife a curious kitty may discover – and an abundance of cattails."

Artist: Sue Horton, Franksville, Wisconsin

A Chicago native, Sue Horton earned a bachelor of science degree from Loyola University of Chicago. After residing in Dusseldorf, Germany, for three years because of her husband's job assignment, she became a full-time homemaker devoting time to her art. Recent projects include murals, painting bisqueware, drawing landscapes and portraits, and creating Hakuna Mutt Tata for Racine's Dog Days of Summer 2002.

Sponsor: The Horton Family

Catquarium

"The housecat's body becomes the magical world of a fish aquarium."

Artist: Deborah Madigan, West Salem, Ohio

Originally from Racine, Deborah Madigan received her bachelor of fine arts degree from Ohio University and her master's degree in library science from Kent State University. She manages a library for the Wayne County Public Library System in Ohio. A multi-media artist, she works with found objects, paint, collage and drawing materials. Her works have been shown in Arizona, New York and the Midwest.

Sponsor: Bukacek Construction, Inc.

Ho (B) Kat

"Simulates the structure of a catamaran using the half pieces of the body for the floats."

Artist: Peg Ducommun, Racine

Peg Ducommun, a Racine resident, has had some of her artwork displayed in Door County, Wisconsin. She has won awards in other shows throughout Wisconsin and Illinois. She loves all forms of art and continues to pursue her passion for the field. Her canine creation was one of the top five in the People's Choice for Dog Days of Summer 2002 in Racine.

Sponsor: Myrna Rae Bellomy

McCatfish

"He loves fish so much he believes he's one too."

Artist: Edith Soghomonian, Racine

A native of France, Edith Soghomonian has lived in Racine for several years. She attended art school and the University of Sciences in France. Oil paintings, articulated models of anatomy and stained glass works are her primary areas of interest in art.

Sponsor: Dorothy Metz – McDonald's

Pussy LaMer
(Cat of the Sea)

"She's half cat, half mermaid."

Artist: Kristina Niemi, Kenosha

Kristina Niemi holds a bachelor of arts and teaching certification from the University of Wisconsin-Parkside. She teaches art at Mahone Middle School in Kenosha, where she is a member of the Lemon Street Gallery. She does painting and drawing on tree slices, and also enjoys print-making, with fish and chickens as her themes. Her hobby is scuba diving.

Sponsor: CTX Mortgage LLC.

Scrubbles

"Diverse sizes, shapes and colors working together result in a pouting but clean Scrubbles."

Artist: Victoria M. Chekouras, Racine

Vicki Chekouras' interest in art started as a child when influenced by her creative father who brought home artist supplies. She was an art major in college. Her passion for art is reflected in tole painting, sketching, stained glass, faux finishes and mural painting. She enjoys reading, gardening and her four cats. She works for SC Johnson as lead computer operator.

Sponsor: St. Lucy's Church

Something Fishy

"Plays on the word 'cat' and cats seem to love fish. Is it a fish or a cat?"

Artists: Tonya Lambeth Dilley and David Dilley, Racine

Something Fishy is a husband-wife collaboration. Tonya received a bachelor of fine arts degree from the University of Wisconsin. Her works range from oil paintings to fiber projects and the occasional crayon project with their young son. Dave is a professionally trained carpenter. He is a woodworker with a specialty in custom musky lures. His interests include musky fishing and deer hunting.

Sponsor: Seater Construction Co., Inc.

The Purrmaid

"The playful feline version of a mermaid."

Artist: Georgene Studey, Racine

Union Grove native Georgene Studey recently moved to Racine and is employed at Alloc, Inc. A lifelong art enthusiast, she completed painting classes at University of Wisconsin-Parkside and now paints and sells many of her items as a hobby. She hopes to pass her love of the arts on to her six-year-old son Hans, who "helps" with many of her paintings.

Sponsor: Alloc, Inc.

33

The Owl and the Pussycat

"Is it an owl or a pussycat?"

Artist: Janet Hanson, Salem, Wisconsin

Janet Hanson received art training during high school and at the University of Wisconsin-Whitewater. Currently she can be found working as an emergency room nurse at All Saints Healthcare System. Her achievements include the accessorising of a log home in London, England, the design of the Union Grove/Yorkville Fire Department centennial logo and murals at All Saints and the Gold Bear.

Sponsor: Racine Emergency Physicians

Cat-loving Celebrations

Cats love celebrations of their own creation. These 13 felines show how to have fun – everything from special vacations to enjoyable times at home.

"Cats do not have to be shown how to have a good time, for they are unfailing ingenious in that respect."

James Mason

A Cat'n Summer Vacation

"He's here for The Big One."

Artist: Violet O'Dell, Racine

Violet O'Dell is an independent artist working in various media, with a three-dimensional emphasis. Though mostly self-taught, she took courses at Wustum Museum of Fine Arts during her high school years. She also attended the University of Wisconsin-Parkside. Most of her works have been privately commissioned. She presently is branching out into public works through her own studio, BrokenWing.

Sponsor: Racine County Convention and Visitors Bureau

Bewitched

"A Halloween inspiration."

Artist: Julie Lynam, Racine

Julie Lynam attended the University of Wisconsin-Stout and earned a degree in art education. She now teaches art and is the student activities director at St. Catherine's High School, Racine. Her favorite medium is painting on canvas. She also enjoys rubber stamping and scrapbooking.

Sponsor: Goebel Electric, Inc.

Birdwatchers at the Castle of Catnappers

"Bird observers quietly enter the castle to view the napping cats."

Artist: Bill Reid, Racine

Nationally known sculptor Bill Reid received his bachelor of fine arts degree from Kansas City (Missouri) Art Institute and his master's degree in fine arts from Cranbook Academy of Art in Bloomfield Hills, Michigan. A graduate of Racine's Prairie School, he also studied at Lawrence University in Appleton and in its program in London, England.

Sponsor: Sam and Gene Johnson

Cat and Mouse Game

"Join in the fun and celebrate the game."

Artist: LeeAnn Morelli, Racine

LeeAnn Morelli has been a commercial artist and graphic designer for more than 25 years, 17 of which have been with CNH/Case Corporation. A lifelong resident of Racine, she is a graduate of Layton School of Art, Milwaukee. Morelli, a devoted animal lover, does fine art in her spare time.

Sponsor: CNH

Cat's Delights

"A depiction of the cat's main areas of interest – catnip grass, small rodents, birds and fish."

Artist: Kristin Gjerdset, Milwaukee

An assistant professor of art at Wisconsin Lutheran College, Milwaukee, Kristin Gjerdset has exhibited her work regionally and nationally. Last summer, she was involved in the Milwaukee Symphony's Beastie Beat public art project. In 2000 she was an artist-in-residence at Glacier National Park in Montana. She has traveled to Norway, California, Washington and Florida to visually preserve the environment through drawings and paintings.

Sponsor: Educators Credit Union

Catz Galore

"Enjoying the out-of-doors and a comfortable bench."

Artists: Daun Johnson and Kim Nelson, Franksville, and Union Grove High School Students

The artists, led by Daun Johnson and Kim Nelson, are students at Union Grove High School. Their prior artistic endeavors include designing and decorating the Enchanted Rainforest Tree for Racine's Festival of Trees in 2002. Johnson is an Alverno College graduate and Nelson is a local artist. Together with these extraordinary students they enjoy creating art projects for the benefit of the community.

Sponsor: Skipper Bud's Reefpoint Marina

Mardi Gras Meow

"Mardi Gras inspired theatrical cat."

**Artists: Pat Levine, Racine, and
Rebekah Levine, Chicago**

Pat Levine and daughter Rebekah Levine have major
artistic achievements to their credit. Pat Levine is an
interior designer who has won national design awards.
She is a professional member of the American Society
of Interior Designers. Rebekah Levine received her
bachelor of fine arts degree from the School of the
Art Institute of Chicago, where she began her master's
program in modern art history in September 2002.
Her preferred media are photography and video.
Her works have been exhibited throughout the
United States and in Mexico.

Sponsor: Waters Edge Clothiers

Kitty Cat Carousel

"Ride the carousel with a bright, elegant cat."

Artist: Kelly Drumm, Racine

Kelly Drumm, a 2002 graduate of Racine's Horlick High School,
attends the University of Wisconsin-Milwaukee, majoring in journalism
and minoring in art. She has spent four summers working as a young
artist within the Racine Parks, Recreational and Cultural Department's
Main Gallery, where her pieces raised money at the charity
auctions held at the end of each summer.

Sponsor: Johnson Financial Group

Palm Beach Cat

"Enjoying the Florida vegetation."

Artist: Rebecca Bissi-Bloom, Racine

Rebecca Bissi-Bloom holds a bachelor of science degree in textiles from the University of Georgia and a bachelor of fine arts degree in fashion design from the School of the Art Institute of Chicago. She worked for 10 years as a fashion designer in Chicago and Hong Kong. She enjoys donating her talents to The Prairie School Premier.

Sponsor: Mathis Gallery and Frame Shop

Parrothead

"A celebration of life by the water, Jimmy Buffet style."

Artist: George Zaleski

George Zaleski is a part-time artist and full-time Parrothead who began listening to the Carribbean-infused tunes of Jimmy Buffett in the early 1980s. Buffett's message – that life is just a little better by the water – seemed a perfect fit for an exhibit set amidst the breezes of Lake Michigan in Downtown Racine. Zaleski is a radiologist who dabbles in acrylics, oils, watercolors and margaritas.

Sponsor: The Zaleski Family

Right Up My Alley

"This ginger cat celebrates the delights in Downtown Racine."

Artist: Julie Trafton, Milwaukee

Julie Trafton is an art specialist at North Park Elementary School, Racine. She was Youth Art Month Southeast Regional Show co-chair in 1998 and was a recipient of the Helen Patton Continuing Education grant through the Racine Community Foundation. Her art has been exhibited in the Racine-Kenosha K-12 Unified Art Teachers' exhibition at University of Wisconsin-Parkside and at Mount Mary College in Milwaukee.

Sponsor: Britton Road Press

Purr-fect Harmony

"Keep the whole world singing."

Artist: Dorothy Reuter, Kenosha

Dorothy Reuter holds a bachelor of arts degree from the University of Wisconsin-Parkside. A member of the Kenosha Art Association, she recently exhibited at the winter show at the Anderson Arts Center in Kenosha. Her work has appeared in a number of local juried exhibitions.

Sponsor: SPEBSQSA – The Barbershop Harmony Society

Sandy Paws

"Ready to go to the beach and shop
for a few items to celebrate Christmas in July."

Artists: The Elves led by Saint Nick: Jen Andert, Pete Conti, Shelley Kutis, Joni Miller, Phyllis Ong-Caro, Lori Peterson, Jan Willette, Tom Yagelski

These eight friends all work at SC Johnson and live in and around Racine. Although they work with numbers by day, they like to express their creative side when they can. When they're not busy working they like to go out for lunch, dinner, shopping or just Cat'n Around Downtown Racine.

Sponsor: Project Management Associates

Celestial Creations

Why be confined by what's on the planet? These six cats go far beyond earth's limits.

"I believe cats to be spirits come to earth. A cat, I am sure, could walk on a cloud without coming through."

Jules Verne

Cat Dreams

"Wistful, wishful cats on clouds enjoy a sky full of fish, birds and mice."

Artist: Mary Lou Dettmer, Racine

As a multi-media artist, Mary Lou Dettmer is inspired by the rainbow of colors available in paints, crayons, papers, pencils and clay. A retired Western Publishing illustrator and editor, her diverse career includes designing Hallmark cards in Kansas City, freelance work with Jim Henson and his Sesame Street characters, and creating children's books and related products from her New York studio.

Sponsor: M & I Bank

Catch a Falling Star

"Enjoy the planets, stars and galaxies."

Artist: Karen J. Balke, Racine

Karen Balke, who has lived in Racine her entire life, is an oil painter and a woodcarver, and makes miniature furniture and doll houses. She also works in pastels and watercolors, and has a whole house full of her artwork. She made the doll house and furniture found in the pediatrics department at Saint Mary's Medical Center, Racine.

Sponsor: Adecco

Aurora Borealis

*"This muralistic feline dons the spectacular
Northern Lights, along with a few Canadian pines."*

Artist: AnnMarie Liesch, Franksville

AnnMarie Liesch is 16 years old and a junior at Case High School. She runs cross country and track. Aside from running, she spends her time outside or reading or painting/remaking model horses. At home she has a not-so-smart yet lovable basset hound and ironically is not fond of cats.

Sponsor: JohnsonDiversey

Cats Are Angels with Fur

"Are they really angels?"

Artist: Laura K. Covelli, Racine

Racine native Laura Covelli graduated from the University of Wisconsin-Stout in December 2002. She holds a bachelor of fine arts degree with a graphic design concentration. A 1998 Case High School graduate, Covelli studied in London in the summer of 2000. She has been entering art shows since her senior year in high school. Her preferred media are pencils, pastels and oil pastels.

Sponsor: Racine Veterinary Hospital

Catsandra the Celestial Princess

"This princess is finished in gold, silver and copper metallics, adorned with brass and beads."

Artist: Deirdre Lapinski, Racine

Deirdre Lapinski has a bachelor of science degree in nursing from the University of Wisconsin-Milwaukee. Art has always been part of her life, and sewing has been her primary medium. She began beading activities about three years ago and that now continues to occupy her free time. She created a canine for 2002's Dog Days of Summer in Racine.

Sponsor: Salute Italian Restaurant

The Dreamer

"This housecat fantasizes about his origins and life in a wild, untamed land."

Artist: Abby McCague, Ottawa, Illinois

Abby McCague is a freelance artist who specializes in murals. She received her education at Harper Rainer Junior College and the School of the Art Institute, Chicago. Currently she is creating an impressionist series of florals for a medical complex and illustrating a children's book. Most of her works are private commissions for small businesses and homes.

Sponsor: Dave and Sandy Trumbo

Culinary Characters

Food is never far away from the mind of a cat. These seven adaptations give that reality some new twists.

"Your cat may never have to hunt farther than the kitchen counter for its supper."

Barbara L. Diamond

47

Cat Chow Made to Purrfection

"Better than the dry stuff out of the bag."

Artist: Don Danowski, Racine

Don Danowski is recognized as one of Wisconsin's top watercolor artists and is well-known nationally for his nature and wildlife paintings. Especially popular are his Midnight Series, featuring animals in their natural moonlit habitats, and his Spirit Series of animals with ghosted images as reminders of their endangerment. Danowski has won numerous awards for his talent.

Sponsor: Courtyard Catering by Spiegelhoff's

48

Kitchen Kitty

"At your service. What will it be?"

Artists: Kristina Niemi, Kenosha, and Marcia Sykes, Racine

Kristina Niemi holds a bachelor of arts and teaching certification from the University of Wisconsin-Parkside. She teaches art at Mahone Middle School in Kenosha and is a member of the Lemon Street Gallery. Marcia Sykes, a teacher in Racine Unified, holds a bachelor of arts degree from University of Wisconsin-Parkside and a master's degree from National Louis University.

Sponsor: Nu-Wood Cabinet, Ltd.

Pickle Puss

"The pickle-lover's pussycat."

Artist: Sandra Bodnar, Racine

Sandra Bodnar graduated from William Horlick High School. For the past 26 years she has been with SC Johnson as a machine operator. She designed the 2001 Fourth of July parade float for SC Johnson. Although she likes pen and ink, she hopes to pursue oil painting in the future. Landscapes and still life are her favorites.

Sponsor: Jay and Ric Ruffo

Purr-fect Dinner

"There's nothing better."

Artist: Joan Houlehen, Cudahy, Wisconsin

A graphic artist/designer, Joan Houlehen is a partner in A. Houberbocken, Inc., an art consulting firm. Her works are in the Northwestern Mutual art collection and many other commercial and private collections. She is a docent at the Haggerty Museum of Art on the Marquette University campus and on the board of directors of the Friends of the Museum.

Sponsor: Johnson Polymer

Sourpuss

"Wouldn't you be a bit sour if the hair on your body was made of lemons?"

Artist: Teresa M. Meyers, Racine

Born and raised in Racine County, Teresa Meyers has loved art since childhood. She expresses this through drawing, theater and now in the form of Sourpuss. She hand-draws her own Christmas cards and for other occasions, cards are done on request. She has worked at Porters of Racine for the past two years. The inspiration for her citrus creation came from her four felines.

Sponsor: Porters of Racine

Sue-Shi

"All set for a gourmet treat."

Artist: Lorie Dana, Racine

Lorie Dana is a third-year undergraduate student at the University of Wisconsin-Parkside. Her majors are music performance and studio art. She has been an active artist her entire life, in drawing, painting and sculpting. She is an oboist and plays in the Racine Concert Band and the University of Wisconsin-Parkside wind ensemble.

Sponsor: The Chartroom

When the Cat's a Whey the Mice Will Play

"A total cheese treat – for the mice."

Artist: Amy Zahalka, Wind Lake, Wisconsin

Amy Zahalka received her art degree from the University of Wisconsin-Madison. During the years she has worked in graphics and visual merchandising. Since returning to the Midwest, she earned her teaching certificate from the University of Wisconsin-Milwaukee and began teaching art in Racine. She has had one show in Milwaukee and recently illustrated a children's book.

Sponsor: Friends of Racine Heritage Museum

Cultured Cats

Cats can be cultured creatures when so inclined. These 23 cover the range from literature to art, music, film and even the newspaper.

"The smallest feline is a masterpiece."

Leonardo da Vinci

Artistocat

"Famous and not so famous artwork has been 'purrfectly' copycatted in collage form to create this cultured kitty cat."

Artists: Debra DeKeuster, Franksville, and Meeka Droese, Racine
Debra DeKeuster teaches art at Racine Lutheran High School. She has also taught in the Racine Unified School District and was the "Outreach 4" coordinator at Charles A. Wustum Museum of Fine Arts. She received a bachelor of fine arts degree from the University of Colorado, majoring in art education and minoring in art history. Meeka Droese is a student at Lutheran High School.

Sponsor: Lutheran High School Booster Club

Cat Gut

"Converted into a stringed instrument."

Artist: Barbara Lindquist, Racine
Barbara Lindquist has been an artist for nearly 70 years. At 14, she was chosen to attend the Chicago Art Institute. At 18, she apprenticed to a violinmaker and she has been making musical instruments since then. She works in all media and her creations are in private collections worldwide. A partner in Mother Courage Press, she has helped produce 25 books.

Sponsor: Olympia Brown Unitarian Universalist Women's Federation.

Cat in Rousseau's Dream

"Henri Rousseau's perfect feline vision."

Artist: Deborah Bartelt, Oshkosh, Wisconsin

Deborah Bartelt has been an elementary art teacher in the Oshkosh Area School District since 1973. She earned her bachelor's degree in art education at the University of Wisconsin-Oshkosh and her master's degree in adaptive art education from St. Norbert College, DePere. Her special skills include watercolors, paper making and sketch journals.

Sponsor: Millers Flowers

Cat-n-Hook

"When you think of water, boats and ships, Captain Hook comes to mind."

Artist: Sara Stewart, Racine

Sara Stewart, a senior at Horlick High School, has participated for several years in the Main Gallery Young Artists Program sponsored by the City of Racine. She and other students also worked on an 82-by-12 foot mural at the Imperial Apartments retirement complex. Stewart plans to attend Milwaukee Institute of Art and Design.

Sponsor: Palmer Johnson Yachts

CatGoyle

"The cat as a gargoyle."

**Artists: Stephanie Andersen and
Blake Thompson, Racine**

Stephanie Andersen is currently working in research
and development at a Milwaukee-based
industrial coatings company. She enjoys
photography in her spare time and created a
dog for last year's Dog Days of Summer.
Thompson is a computer programmer who expresses his
creativity in the Web sites he both designs and manages.

Sponsor: First Stepp Builders

Catman

"A cat kind of like Batman."

**Artists: Waylon Nielsen, Phil Williams and
R.E.A.L. School Students, Racine**

Waylon Nielsen is a student at the R.E.A.L. School, Racine. This 14-year-
old's favorite classes are math and art. He also likes to play his Xbox and
PS2. He was assisted by his art teacher, Phil Williams, another eighth
grader, Kyle Jorgenson, and other R.E.A.L. School students.

Sponsor: Ricky's Place

Chat des Seurat

"Painted in the pointillist style of French artist Georges Seurat."

Artist: Tina Parise-Mitchell, West Bend, Wisconsin
Racine native Tina Parise-Mitchell earned her bachelor of arts degree in visual arts from the University of Wisconsin-Milwaukee in May 2003, with an emphasis in painting and ceramics. Her work has been exhibited in numerous shows and competitions. An image of one of her sculptures was featured on the cover of the UW-Milwaukee Union Art Gallery calendar.

Sponsor: Knight-Barry Title, Inc.

Clawed Monet

"Colors blended in the style of Claude Monet."

Artists: Lory Froncek, Racine, and Nancy Froncek, Madison, Wisconsin
For the past 40 years, Lory Froncek has taken periodic classes at the Charles A. Wustum Museum of Fine Arts. She paints with the senior painting group at Chavez Center in Racine and has had acrylic paintings accepted for many Racine Art Guild shows. Her niece, Nancy Froncek, has been a food stylist entrepreneur of Professional Kitchen in Madison since 1983.

Sponsor: Tri City National Bank

DeClaude Mewnet

"Claude Monet's works inspired this cat."

Artists: Christine Sretenovich and Wind Point Elementary School Third Grade Students, Racine

Christine Sretenovich, art teacher at Wind Point Elementary School, and her third graders created DeClaude Mewnet. A bachelor of fine arts graduate from the University of Wisconsin-Whitewater, Sretenovich has been with Racine Unified School District since 1989. After extensive study of Claude Monet and the impressionism style, the students worked with Sretenovich to create their impression of Monet's water lilies, haystacks and figures.

Sponsor: The Kiefer Family

Feline Groovy

"The cat borrows the song and flower-child motif of the sixties."

Artist: Theresa Schiffer, Racine

A graduate of the University of Wisconsin-Parkside with a major in fine art, Theresa Schiffer currently works as a feature artist for the *Milwaukee Journal Sentinel*. Prior to that, she was the design editor for *The Journal Times*, Racine. She has won numerous design awards, both international and state, during her career in newspapers.

Sponsor: Patricia Jander

Hemingway Cat — Charlie Chaplin

"This cat is one of the dozens who lives at Hemingway's Key West home."

Artist: Kristin Gjerdset, Milwaukee

An assistant professor of art at Wisconsin Lutheran College, Milwaukee, Kristin Gjerdset has exhibited her work regionally and nationally. Last summer, she was involved in the Milwaukee Symphony's Beastie Beat public art project. In 2000 she was an artist-in-residence at Glacier National Park in Montana. She has traveled to Norway, California, Washington and Florida to visually preserve the environment through drawings and paintings.

Sponsor: Knight-Barry Title, Inc.

Jellicle Cat

"Students at the Dance Arts Center chose the name for this cat."

Artist: Danelle Schultz, Franksville

Danelle Schultz is the owner/director of Dance Arts Center, Franksville. She holds the title of Mrs. Wisconsin 2002 and enjoyed making the majority of her title appearances in the Downtown Racine area. Her other artistic interests include painting and decorating. Jellicle Cat is a representation of her love for dance and theater. The musical *Cats* was the first Broadway production she ever attended.

Sponsor: Dance Arts Center/The Hair Connection

Meowlyn Monroe

*"Presenting that fabulous feline
from the fifties, a purrfect American beauty."*

Artist: Jayne Miner, Racine
Jayne Miner has been an art teacher for Racine Unified schools the past 24 years. She currently teaches at Case High School. She has her bachelor of arts degree from Calvin College and her master's degree from Carthage College. Miner enjoys creating watercolor paintings and art metals. She also created The Wizard of Dogz for Dog Days of Summer 2002.

Sponsor: Sierra Inc.

Paw.lez-vous français?

"All things French come to Downtown Racine."

Artist: Lois Van Liew, Thiensville, Wisconsin
Lois Van Liew holds a bachelor of art education degree from the University of Kansas in Lawrence, and has done advanced study at the University of Missouri and Ox-Bow in Saugatuck, Michigan. She has participated in many juried and invitational exhibits and won numerous awards for her work. Her works appear in many public and private collections.

Sponsor: Thermal Transfer Products

Pic "Cat" so

"This artist really gets into his work."

Artist: Amy J. Davis, Racine

Amy Davis and her family moved to Racine in July 2002. Originally from Ohio, she has an associate degree in graphic design. Her preferred media are pencil, and pen and ink with watercolor wash. She enjoys trying new things in the way of homemade crafts. Her first love, however, is singing, dating to her childhood.

Sponsor: Crossroads Animal Hospital

Puss in Boots

"The children's story is the perfect inspiration for this cat."

Artist: Laura Underwood, Caledonia

A graduate of the fine arts program at Murray State University in Murray, Kentucky, Laura Underwood is a freelance illustrator and fine artist. She illustrates using primarily pastels and has had her work shown in Chicago galleries. She currently creates out of her home studio in Caledonia.

Sponsor: Design Partners, Inc.

Sagwa: the Chinese Siamese Cat

"The popular character from the PBS children's show and Amy Tan's book."

Artists: Kelly Gallaher, Racine, and Children from Families with Children from China/Racine Chapter

Kelly Gallaher has been an active artist in residence in the Racine area for almost a decade. Working in a variety of media – from ceramics to metal sculpture, murals and mosaics – Gallaher specializes in creating large-scale art events for school-age children. About 12 children helped create Sagwa.

Sponsor: D. J. Kontra, M.D. and Associates, S.C.

Tabbey Road

"Painted to resemble the Beatles' album, 'Abbey Road,' along with other Beatles' images."

Artist: Paul Muckler, Oak Creek, Wisconsin

As a youngster Milwaukee native Paul Muckler showed his love of art with pencils, crayons and watercolors. Horizons have expanded and he holds several degrees from the University of Wisconsin-Milwaukee and Milwaukee Area Technical College. Interests include landscapes, still life, portraiture and art work of all types. The Beatles are among his many personal heroes.

Sponsor: Adecco Technical

The Cat's in the Ladle

"A spoof on the popular song, 'The Cat's in the Cradle.'"

Artist: Randall Underwood, Caledonia

Randall Underwood is a graphic designer who recently relocated to the Racine area after working in Chicago since graduation from Drake University in 1986. His degree is in advertising media graphics. He currently is a creative director for Design Partners, Inc., in Downtown Racine.

Sponsor: Design Partners, Inc.

The Cheshire Cat

"No matter what curious things are going on around him, the Cheshire Cat of Wonderland remains tranquil and unbothered."

Artist: Melanie Pope, Racine

Melanie Pope is a graduate of the University of Wisconsin-Whitewater, with a bachelor of fine arts degree. She is currently painting murals in businesses, homes and schools, and is planning to serve as an artist-in-residence. Her entry in Downtown Racine's Dog Days of Summer event in 2002 received third place. She looks forward to writing and illustrating children's books some day.

Sponsor: Racine Public Library

The Cheshire Cat

"This feline is adorned with characters from Alice in Wonderland."

Artist: Amy Zahalka, Wind Lake, Wisconsin

Amy Zahalka received her art degree from the University of Wisconsin-Madison. During the years she has worked in graphics and visual merchandising. Since returning to the Midwest, she earned her teaching certificate from the University of Wisconsin-Milwaukee and began teaching art in Racine. She has had one show in Milwaukee and recently illustated a children's book.

Sponsor: Racine Family YMCA

Vasily "Kat"insky 1911

"Done in a style befitting Vasily Kandinsky's work; color conveys movement and emotion."

Artist: Rosemary Curtin, Racine

Born and raised in North Carolina near the Outer Banks, Rosemary Curtin feels at home with Lake Michigan in her backyard. Her studies include courses at the Milwaukee Institute of Art and Design and workshops with artists here and in Pennsylvania. Her work is influenced by V. Kandinsky and S. McDonald-Wright, who used emotions of color in their work.

Sponsor: Nader Salti, M.D.

What's News, Pussycat?

"Catching up on the daily newspaper."

Artist: Karen Johnston, Racine

Janesville native Karen Johnston received her bachelor's degree in art education from the University of Wisconsin-Madison and her masters of fine arts from Southern Illinois University-Carbondale, where she taught for two years. She also has taught art in K-12 settings, and was adjunct instructor at the University of Wisconsin-Parkside. Her ceramic sculptures have been exhibited in several Midwestern shows.

Sponsor: *The Journal Times*

Feline Fashions

The majesty and beauty of the cat lends itself to all types of adornment and adaptation, as these 23 beauties prove.

"*Just as the would-be debutante will fret and fuss over every detail till all is perfect, so will the fastidious feline patiently toil until every whiskertip is in place.*"

Lynn Hollyn

Button Bob

"Button, button, who has the button?"

**Artists: Kayla Cacciotti, Phil Williams and
R.E.A.L. School Students, Racine**
Kayla Cacciotti is a seventh-grade student at the R.E.A.L. School, Racine.
She loves art and has taken art classes since first grade. She was assisted by
her art teacher, Phil Williams, and other R.E.A.L. School students.

Sponsor: The R.E.A.L. School

Cat 'n Hats

"Hats for every occasion."

Artist: Sybil Brauneis Klug, Lake Geneva, Wisconsin
Fontana Elementary School teacher Sybil Brauneis Klug works
in acrylics and oils. Color is the primary focus of her landscapes,
flowers and still-life arrangements. Her paintings have been included
in juried shows at the Charles A. Wustum Museum of Fine Arts,
Anderson Arts Center in Kenosha and Rotary Gardens in Janesville.
Her work can be seen at the GLAA Gallery in Lake Geneva.

Sponsor: Nordik of America

Cat Eyes

"There's no escaping this cat's uncanny cat's eye view."

Artists: DeeDee Dumont and Mickie Krueger, Racine

Both DeeDee Dumont and Mickie Krueger are active in the Racine and Kenosha area arts communities. Their works have appeared in many shows and are in private collections. Dumont's professional career is focused on graphic arts; she currently is the graphic artist/designer and photographer for Milaeger's, Inc. Krueger's job experiences include silkscreen instructor, graphic artist, marketing assistant and other freelance work.

Sponsor: Accents on Main

Cat with a "Mousey" Brown Coat

"Mice in a variety of poses adorn this cat's coat."

Artist: Carla Marie Reed, Fall River, Wisconsin

Carla Reed holds a bachelor of science degree in nursing from Marian College in Fond du Lac, Wisconsin. She enjoys quilting, cross-stitch, sketching, drawing and painting. She has even attempted a woodcarving with a chainsaw. She also has home remodeling talents such as tiling, wall-papering, stenciling and even drywalling. This is her first public art attempt.

Sponsor: W. H. Pugh

Cat's Eye

"Marbles make the perfect covering."

Artists: Jim Jr. and Nancy Tyyska, Racine

This mother-son duo works in a variety of media. Nancy Tyyska uses oil as her medium of choice while son Jim works on the computer. Nancy is retired and enjoys travel and crafts. Jim is currently employed by Wisconsin artist Don Nedobeck. He has done art design and direction for various Web sites and also creates art for art's sake.

Sponsor: Johnson-Keland Management, Inc.

Cat's Pajamas

"This Maine Coon cat is ready for bed."

Artist: Cary Hunkel, Madison, Wisconsin

Cary Hunkel was educated at the University of Wisconsin-Madison where she earned her master of fine arts degree. She is a member of the Society of Animal Artists, and her watercolors and drawings have been shown throughout North America. She also has illustrated several wildlife books and articles.

Sponsor: Maresh-Meredith and Acklam Funeral Home

Cat's Pajamas

*"Ready to retire in his sleeping finery,
hoping to impress even a casual onlooker."*

Artist: Terrence J. Nolden, Racine

Terrence Nolden has taught art in Racine for the past 15 years. Currently an art specialist at Jefferson Lighthouse Elementary School, he introduces art experiences to students in grades K-5. Additionally, Nolden teaches elementary arts and crafts during summer sessions. Prior to teaching, he was a sales representative for a variety of architectural building products.

Sponsor: Jefferson Lighthouse Elementary School PTA

Catarina

"A crazy quilt fantasy."

Artists: Linda Schubring, Sue Causey and Katy Diekfuss, Racine

Sue Causey has an extensive background in various artistic endeavors, including years as an award-winning quilter. Linda Schubring generates creative ideas to promote and support artistic endeavors. Katy Diekfuss is a talented, enthusiastic and creative artist who also is a cat lover. All participated in 2002's Dog Days of Summer in Downtown Racine.

Sponsor: Coldwell Banker Residential Brokerage

69

Fat Cat

"A beautiful, humorous, very strong 'in your face' Fat Cat conceptual statement."

Artist: Maxine K. Rabinowe, Racine

Interior designer and fine arts consultant Maxine Rabinowe, owner of Homespun Studios© in Racine, received her bachelor of fine arts summa cum laude from the University of Michigan and her CSS from Harvard University. She was also a summer fellow for two seasons at Ox-Bow in Saugatuck, Michigan.

Sponsor: Diabetes Osteoporosis Thyroid Endocrine Centers, LLC

Fat Cat

"Adorned with money and all the trappings."

Artist: Lori Schory, Genoa City, Wisconsin

Lori Schory, a Chicago native, has her masters of fine arts degree from Northern Illinois University. Since 1983 she has been specializing in custom hand lettering and graphics for boats, vans, trucks and signage of all types for theme restaurants and other businesses. She accepts individual commissions for pictorial murals and hand-painted accessories and furniture to coordinate with any environment.

Sponsor: Faye Becker Homes, Inc.

Jewel, the Queen of Racine

"She sparkles and shimmers with a glittery mosaic skin of glitzy recycled jewelry."

Artist: Kate Proeber, Caledonia

Kate Proeber, a University of Wisconsin-Parkside graduate and a native Racinian, has been teaching art at Shoreland Lutheran High School in Somers, Wisconsin, for the past 17 years. Her work has been shown at the Charles A. Wustum Museum of Fine Arts in Racine, the Anderson Art Center in Kenosha, and Rotary Gardens in Janesville. She enjoys drawing, painting, printmaking, found-object art and papermaking.

Sponsor: Vince and JoAnn Sollazo

JoseFeline and Her Amazing Technicolor Dreamcoat

"Her rainbow coat is enhanced with 'ermine' collar and cuffs."

Artist: Julie Pasteur, Racine

Milwaukee native Julie Pasteur has lived in Racine since 1986 and since 1989 has been a deputy family court commissioner. Her law degree is from the University of San Francisco and her undergraduate degree is from Northwestern University. She became interested in working with color and design during a retreat at the Siena Center in Racine.

Sponsor: Lakeview Pharmacy

Kiltie Cat (Cat'n in a Kilt)

*"Kiltie Cat marches wearing a bright smile and inner glow,
a musical salute to Racine's astronaut, Laurel Salton Clark."*

Artist: Lois Caryn Smith, Racine

For more than 30 years, Lois Caryn Smith has attracted public and private collectors with her displays, murals and paintings. She received her bachelor's degree in art and design from the University of Wisconsin-Parkside and mastered in animation under the Disney animators in Toronto, Ontario. She instructs students, both children and adults, in schools and privately.

Sponsor: Dr. Robert and Susan Siegert

Majestic Murphy

"A cat with a magnificent majestic coat."

Artist: Marilyn C. Benson, Racine

Marilyn Benson has always been creative with her hands – drawing, painting, sewing. She enjoys working in any medium and currently is working as a freelance graphic designer and writer. Her love of animals is exhibited by the work she does on their behalf, including her work with Countryside Humane Society. She also edits and designs Gateway Technical College's student newspaper, *Gateway Gazette*.

Sponsor: Countryside Humane Society

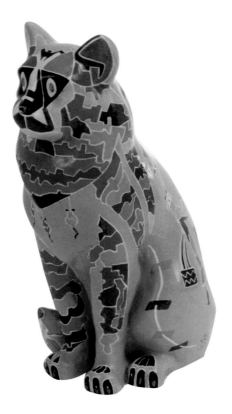

Navajo Sam

"Represents the Southwest."

Artist: Stan Feiker (Gray Wolf), Racine

Stan Feiker, who uses his adopted Indian name "Gray Wolf," has carved and painted wildlife and Southwest Indian art for many years. He also is a wildlife photographer and has his own processing lab.

Sponsor: Phil and Jean Jacobson

Persian Cat

"A Persian rug befits the cat."

Artist: Bonita Carbajal, Racine

A native of Stevens Point, Wisconsin, Bonita Carbajal studied architecture and art history at the University of Wisconsin-Milwaukee. She works in oil, charcoal and watercolor, and does papier maché sculpture using recycled materials such as paper bags. She participated in Dog Days of Summer in Downtown Racine and Festival of Trees, both in 2002.

Sponsor: Chuck and Sue Pehlivanian

Persian Catpet

"Rich jewel colors of the Persian rug."

Artist: Lenore Sydnor, Racine

Lenore Sydnor, a goldsmith and jewelry designer, owns VSO Ltd. in Downtown Racine. She opened her business in 1974, and taught art in Racine Unified schools for seven years. She attended Syracuse University and graduated from the University of Wisconsin-Madison. She did graduate work at the University of Wisconsin-Milwaukee and has completed several G.I.A. workshops. She is currently enjoying learning blacksmithing.

Sponsor: Barbara S. Walter

Pewter Purrfect

"Elegance in a special covering."

Artists: Michael and Vernay Mueller, Racine

Vernay Mueller, a freelance artist, and Michael Mueller, a pipe layer for A. W. Oakes, are native Racinians and avid collectors of antiques and Racine memorabilia. Vernay's works include two- and three-dimensional art pieces as well as decorative furniture and wall finishes. Michael's interests include photography, softball and playing Santa for his grandchildren, nieces and nephews, friends, hospitals and senior centers.

Sponsor: WISPARK LLC

Polka Dot Cat

"The boldly colored dots represent the vibrancy of the city."

Artist: John Ernst, West Allis, Wisconsin

John Ernst exhibits his work primarily in Southeastern Wisconsin galleries. His bold abstract paintings incorporate the vibrant colors that blend and balance the dimensions of depth, animation and texture in an effort to establish an emotional connection with the viewer. He prefers a minimalist approach and strives to create works that evoke strong, positive feelings.

Sponsor: A-1 Auto Body

Rose-Bud

"The Norwegian art form adorns this cat well."

Artist: Janet Piddington, Madison, Wisconsin

Janet Piddington began rosemaling in the early 1980s, loving this folk art from the beginning. She studied with gold-medalist and Norwegian artists and eventually taught through Madison Area Technical College in both Stoughton and Madison for the past 20 years.

Sponsor: Quizno's Downtown

Rosie...Dressed to the Nines

"A touch of class, all dressed up to go Cat'n Around Downtown."

Artist: Cathy McCombs, Racine

Cathy McCombs has taught art at The Prairie School in Racine for the past 20 years. She holds degrees from Layton School of Art, Carthage College and the University of Wisconsin-Milwaukee. Her current artistic love and challenge is glassblowing, adding to her experiences in printmaking, illustration and painting. Her works are in private collections throughout the United States.

Sponsor: Shear Madness

Shatter Glass Kitty

"Mosaic style using shattered tempered glass technique."

Artist: Sherry Lou Martin, Racine

Sherry Lou Martin has been involved with art for the past 20 years. She is an award-winning wood carver, specializing in blue herons and egrets. She also paints wildlife, florals and landscapes. The shatter-glass technique is also one of the media in which she works. Martin's works are shown in several Wisconsin galleries.

Sponsor: Twin Disc, Inc.

Stringing Me Along

"Yarn is the ideal medium to dress a cat."

Artist: Christine R. Polewski, Brookfield, Wisconsin

Racine native Christine Polewski exhibited in Watercolor Wisconsin at Charles A. Wustum Museum of Fine Arts, as well as many other shows. She's won a number of awards and honors. She is past secretary of the League of Milwaukee Artists and a member of the Midwest Watercolor Society. She does murals for private individuals and corporate clients, and her works are found in many private collections.

Sponsor: Charles and Joan Patton

Historic Happenings

Thousands of years ago cats were revered as deities. It's been said they've never forgotten this. These 17 cats prove that point, while also honoring more recent historic events.

"Cats as a class have never completely got over the snootiness caused by the fact that in Ancient Egypt they were worshipped as gods."

P. G. Wodehouse

Cleo-Catra

"Ornate cat in Cleopatra style."

Artist: Judy K. Yorgan, Racine

Judy Olsen-Yorgan is the owner, designer and goldsmith of Plumb Gold Ltd., in Downtown Racine, the business she established in 1976. She has her bachelor of arts degree from the University of Wisconsin-Parkside. Among her local commissions are works for University of Wisconsin-Parkside, Carthage College, Case-Tenneco Corporation, Unico and The Prairie School.

Sponsor: Plumb Gold Ltd.

Cleo-Kattra
(I Want My Mummy)

"Incorporates the ancient Egyptians' worship of cats and their mummification."

Artist: Robert M. Bleeke II, Oak Creek, Wisconsin

A graduate of Carthage College, Kenosha, with a degree in graphic arts, Bleeke currently works at the Racine Public Library and in the summer also at the Bristol Renaissance Faire. In his spare time he puts his artistic efforts into self-published comic books and children's book ideas.

Sponsor: Racine Public Library

Cleocatra and the Kitten Kingdom

"The queen of cats enthroned reigns above little Egypt with sphinx, pyramids and kittens, of course."

Artist: Karen Johnston, Racine

Janesville native Karen Johnston received her bachelor's degree in art education from the University of Wisconsin-Madison and her masters of fine arts from Southern Illinois University-Carbondale, where she taught for two years. She also has taught art in K-12 settings, and was adjunct instructor at the University of Wisconsin-Parkside. Her ceramic sculptures have been exhibited in several Midwestern shows.

Sponsor: *The Journal Times*

Cleocatra

"Portrays the beauty and majesty of Cleopatra."

Artists: Janet Mrazek, Racine; David Gaura, Franksville; Linda Morafcik, Kenosha

Janet Mrazek, a graphic designer, creates hand-made paper vessels, pastels and watercolors. David Gaura is an oil painter and sculptor, working in wood, metal and glass. Linda Morafcik is a graphic designer and fiber artist. Fostered by their association as Racine Art Guild members, all three are eager to work in new art forms – such as cat sculpture!

Sponsor: Aurora Health Care

Cleocatra: Dressed to Impress

"Egyptian cat gleaming with gold and jewels."

Artists: Katie Gebhardt and Christie Helding, Racine

Both Katie Gebhardt and Christie Helding are students at Washington Park High School, Racine. Katie is also involved in the city's Main Gallery program and helped create a dog for last year's Dog Days of Summer in Racine. Christie is artistically talented and loves to do art in her spare time.

Sponsor: Park High School/PTSA

Coppurrnicus Cat

"Follows the theories of 15th century Polish astronomer Nicholas Copernicus."

Artist: Marj Lacock, Racine

Marj Lacock received her fine arts degree from the University of Wisconsin-Parkside. She currently works with watercolors on paper or canvas, enhancing the images with colored pencils, metallic leaf and beads. Her works have appeared in many Southeastern Wisconsin invitational and juried exhibitions. She is a member of Artists Gallery, Racine, and Seebeck Gallery, Kenosha.

Sponsor: Wisconsin Health and Fitness of Racine, LLC

Egypt's Pride

"Adorned with dressings from classic Egyptian art; burial headpiece of King Tut; collar and cuffs from bust of Queen Nefratiti."

Artists: Joseph and Heather Brayer, Sturtevant

Joseph and Heather Brayer met in art classes at the University of Wisconsin-Parkside. Now Joseph, an information technology analyst for Snap-on, and Heather, a stay-at-home mom, use their artistic talent for personal enjoyment and for various volunteer projects at Evangelical United Methodist Church. Their common art interests range from photography and graphic design to textiles, sculpture and painting.

Sponsor: Oasis Vending

Jinx the Sphinx

"Truly a monument, complete with hieroglyphics."

Artist: Judith Koenig, Racine

A self-taught artist, Judith Koenig has no formal art training. Her art consists of abstract impressionism and mixed media. She expresses her creativity not only through canvas art but with music, poetry, acting and fashion design.

Sponsor: Norman and Lynne Monson

Kitty Hawk — The Wright Cat

"A play on the name of the place where the Wright Brothers achieved their first flight."

Artist: Trudi Theisen, Monona, Wisconsin

Kitty Hawk, a centennial tribute to flight, is of real interest to the artist. Her husband is a retired airline employee. This year, 2003, commemorates the 100-year anniversary of flight. Trudi Theisen graduated from the University of Wisconsin-Madison. She has participated in numerous juried exhibitions throughout Wisconsin, Wyoming and Arizona.

Sponsor: Jim and Roberta Fiene

Kitty Hawk

"One-hundredth anniversary of the first flight at Kitty Hawk, North Carolina."

Artist: Russell E. Asala, Racine

Russell Asala, a graduate of Northwestern University, began his career at SC Johnson and subsequently owned two art and design studios: Creative Concepts, Inc., and Phoenix Design Group, Inc. While now retired, Asala does substitute teaching at the elementary school level. Among his hobbies are art, cooking and gardening.

Sponsor: Photographic Design, Ltd.

Kittyhawk

"Commemorates the Wright Brothers' contribution to America's history of innovation."

Artist: Candace Walters, Racine

Candace Walters is a graphic design graduate of the Rhode Island School of Design. She is currently specializing in brand and package design and has a love for sculpture in all forms of media.

Sponsor: Design Partners, Inc.

Louis Quatorze

"A tribute to French King Louis XIV, who devoted his reign to making France the cultural center of the world."

Artist: Flo Walker, Wautoma, Wisconsin

Flo Walker follows folk art tradition in that, with little formal training, she finds expression in a variety of art, from calligraphy, design and mixed media through oil portraits, landscapes and murals. She has received awards for portraits, photography and mixed media. Her artwork fills the niches and spaces around family, home, office and community.

Sponsor: Landmark Title of Racine, Inc.

Mummy

"An adaptation of the cats found mummified in the tombs of Egypt."

Artist: Kendra Bulgrin, Franksville

Kendra Bulgrin is a junior at the University of Wisconsin-Whitewater, majoring in art with emphasis on drawing and painting, and minoring in Japanese. After graduating from Case High School she spent a year in Japan, studying Asian arts and culture. She hopes to return to Asia to teach English and become a working artist.

Sponsor: Joe and Terri Maier

Pharaoh

"This sculptured piece captures history as a fine-art museum piece."

Artist: Jay Harris, Tichigan, Wisconsin

Jay Harris is a Chicago-born artist currently working as a graphic designer in Downtown Racine. A graduate of Northern Illinois University with degrees in both art and philosophy, he devotes most of his free time to writing and performing music with his band, WesternGrand. He and his family enjoy country living.

Sponsor: Design Partners, Inc.

Purrasaurus

"A prehistoric cat – mostly skin like a dinosaur but fluffy fur around its face."

Artist: Kathy Perkins, Racine

Kathy Perkins began to learn art from her father, a commercial artist and sculptor. She later attended Carthage College and then the University of Wisconsin-Parkside, earning a bachelor of arts degree in fine arts. She is currently employed at SC Johnson as a graphic designer, where she has earned an award for product development. Kayaking is her favorite pastime.

Sponsor: SC Johnson A Family Company

RocKat

*"Cave-painting-like surface, to make it appear
like some ancient artifact left behind."*

Artist: Colleen Johnson, Caledonia

Caledonia native Colleen Johnson attended the University of Wisconsin-
Green Bay and received her bachelor of fine arts from the University of
Wisconsin-Milwaukee, with majors in painting and drawing, and
graphic design. A graphic designer in Racine, she is married and has
one- and three-year-old sons who also left their "paw prints" on
RocKat. Johnson's interest in prehistoric cave paintings inspired RocKat.

Sponsor: Katt Construction Co., Inc.

The Sacred Cat

"Praise to thee, O Ra…thou art the great cat, the avenger of the gods."

Artist: Erica Anderson, Madison, Wisconsin

Erica Anderson attended the University of Wisconsin in Madison, where
she studied art with a concentration in graphic design while majoring
in English literature. She currently lives and works in Madison.

Sponsor: Brian and Joyce Anderson

Purrfect Professionals

While cats as a species are not known for their consistent productive energies, these 15 do take into consideration the world of work.

"The great charm of cats is their rampant egotism, their devil-may-care attitude toward responsibility, their disinclination to earn an honest dollar."

Robertson Davies

Baron

"The cat as a landlord, equipped with all the right tools and supplies."

Artist: Keri Ciesielski, Racine

A graduate of Horlick High School, Keri Ciesielski received her bachelor of fine arts degree in drawing from Arizona State University. After returning to Racine, she discovered her love for teaching. She now teaches art at St. Lucy School and Sacred Heart School, where she applies all aspects of art. She believes art is a fun and relaxing form of expression and communication.

Sponsor: Southern Wisconsin Landlords Association

Callicat

"Calligraphy and ornamental lettering, all referring to the 'cat.' "

Artist: Daryl Redekopp, Racine

Originally from Canada, Daryl Redekopp lived in West Virginia before moving to Racine in January of 1999. Introduced to calligraphy in 1980, he has used this art to create and sell hundreds of beautifully designed pieces. He is a member of the Cream City Calligraphers and the Racine Art Guild and has taught calligraphy classes for many years.

Sponsor: Hartmann Design, Inc.

Cat-a-ma-Ram

"This cat is the committed RAM shopper, who shops until she drops."

Artists: Lisa Englander and RAM Store Staff, Racine

Lisa Englander is the manager of the Racine Art Museum store and a nationally known painter. Her remarkable retail feline staff of kitty wranglers and cat painters includes Cassandra Coley, Caroline Murphy, Sarah Nielsen, Patty Roberson and Michael Filimowicz. The shopping bags are courtesy of Mark Nielsen, bag maker to the Cat-a-ma-RAM.

Sponsor: Sebastian's Fine Food and Spirits

Catouflage

"An elite team with nine lives."

Artist: Timothy Carls, Racine

A Racine native and a University of Wisconsin-Parkside graduate, Timothy Carls is a fine artist and graphic designer who has been involved in the Downtown revitalization since 1996. His design was chosen for the Sixth Street Heart of the Arts banners. He also provides logo designs, graphics and signage for local businesses.

Sponsor: Carpetland USA

Catscan

"The results of a full-body x-ray."

Artist: Megan Clausen, Racine

A senior at Washington Park High School, Megan Clausen hopes to attend college out west and study for an art degree after high school graduation. She enjoys many types of art to expand her options for creativity. The biggest influence in her artistic pursuits is her grandmother, who has taught her how to perfect her talents and motivated her to be the best she can be.

Sponsor: Beechwood Veterinary Clinic

Copy Cat

"Polymer clay, impressed with hard-copy printing plates from newspapers, was used to create this cat."

Artist: J. S. Adams, Racine

A lifelong Racine resident and mixed-media artist, James Adams also has a strong interest in digital fine art. He received his art education at Layton School of Art in Milwaukee, and is a member of Charles A. Wustum Museum Art Association and Wisconsin Painters and Sculptors. He is also a mail carrier in West Racine.

Sponsor: Robert W. Baird

Cop 'n Kiddies

"Reflects Racine's Cops 'n Kids reading program."

Artists: Sr. Janet Weyker and Friends, Racine
Educated at St. Catherine's High School and
Dominican College in Racine, Sr. Janet
Weyker, OP, earned a master's degree
in art education at the University of
Wisconsin-Madison. Helping her
with Cop 'n Kiddies were
Barbara Hagman, Dorothy
Knoedler, Susan Liedel, Susan
Ramagli, Judy Walthers and Rebecca Walthers,
all members of Quota International.

Sponsor: Quota International of Kenosha-Racine

92

Copy Cat

"Cats, cats and more cats."

Artist: Tim Baumstark, Racine

Tim Baumstark holds a bachelor of fine arts degree from the Milwaukee Institute of Art and Design. Currently an art director at Bellwether Communications, he is the owner of Boxhead Design, a graphic design studio in Racine. Baumstark enjoys working three-dimensionally.

Sponsor: Korndoerfer Development

Cowboy Kitty

"All set to work on the range."

Artists: Lance and Jan Steimle, Racine

Racine natives Lance and Jan Steimle found designing a cat an exciting way to have fun working together and exploring their creativity. Lance, an aspiring artist, enjoys working on his newly acquired drawing and painting skills while Jan, a former crafter currently employed at Johnson Bank, figures out the materials needed to complete the design theme.

Sponsor: Dick and Kathy Hansen

Kitty of Industry

"A theme of industry and construction, reflecting the working-class roots of the Racine area."

Artist: Christopher Dembroski, Chicago

A Racine native, Christopher Dembroski graduated from the Milwaukee Institute of Art and Design. He also has studied painting at the Studio Art Center International in Florence, Italy, and has been a guest at the Lacoste School of the Arts in Lacoste, France. He has worked in many art-related fields, from mural work to interior design.

Sponsor: E. C. Styberg Engineering Co.

Meowscles

"True professional grit – when it comes to working out and building those muscles."

Artist: Jeff Levonian, Racine

Jeff Levonian graduated from University of Wisconsin-Parkside with a bachelor of arts degree in art. He's currently employed at Speedtech International, Inc., and also enjoys coaching soccer at Horlick High School. After the overwhelming success of Dog Days of Summer, he decided to create a cat. Family members helped him braid the yarn that forms the cat's muscle structure.

Sponsor: Dimple's Fine Imports

Pole Cat

"Need a haircut?"

Artist: Robert W. Andersen, Racine

A Racine native, Robert Andersen has been an art teacher in the Racine Unified School District since 1972 and an active local artist for three decades. A graduate of Park High School, he received his bachelor of science degree in art from the University of Wisconsin-Whitewater and his master's degree in education from Carthage College.

Sponsor: Captain's Chair

Professor Charley Barleycorn Returns to School

"Charley is a working cat who loves his jobs as much as he is loved by the people he visits."

Artist: Juds Connell, Racine

A painter, sculptor and performance artist, Juds Connell lives in Racine with her art and her cats. As a Countryside Humane Society volunteer, she manages its education and community outreach programs, is its webmaster, and writes the column, Happy Tails, for *Renaissance Magazine*.

Sponsor: Countryside Humane Society

Scruffy the Hobo Cat

"He's a wanderer and loves his job."

Artists: Jane Cascio and Main Gallery Artists, Racine

Jane Cascio is a local artist with a bachelor of fine arts degree from Rockford College. Very active in the local arts community, Cascio has had several pieces in juried shows, most recently Watercolor Wisconsin, and is an artist in residence for Racine's Main Gallery program. Students assisting her were Teresa Christensen and Gage Cascio, both Horlick High School juniors.

Sponsor: Donald and Gabriella Klein

Victor

"A symbol for victory over those who want to destroy the United States."

Artist: Jane Thronson, Franksville, Wisconsin

A former teacher of art and stagecraft in the Racine school system, Jane Thronson was also employed by a Chicago advertising agency in the production department and as an artist at University of Wisconsin-Madison designing promotional materials for the continuing education department. Most recently, she is crafting Americana pieces, lawn ornaments and nautical accessories in a variety of media.

Sponsor: Lifeforce Chiropractic S.C.

Pussycat Predicaments

Because of their never-ending curiosity, cats do find themselves in challenging circumstances periodically, many of them of their own making, as these six cats show.

"A cat can purr its way out of anything."

Donna McCrohan

Cat-Chu!

"This kitty has more than just sniffles."

Artists: Jeanne and Ron Shelby, Racine

Jeanne and Ron Shelby have lived in Racine their entire lives. Jeanne has an associate degree in fashion merchandising but her real passion always has been graphic design. A long-time SC Johnson employee, she works in Creative Operations as a graphic designer. Ron studied engineering and drafting at the University of Wisconsin-Madison and University of Wisconsin-Milwaukee. He is the store manager of Automotive Parts in Sturtevant.

Sponsor: The Rooney Girls

Cat-astrophe

"This one has used up eight of his nine lives."

Artists: Ed Dechant and Jerry Daleski, Racine

Ed Dechant and Jerry Daleski are senior graphic artists at SC Johnson. Lifelong residents, they knew since childhood they wanted to be artists. Dechant followed his father in the commercial art field. Daleski recalls taking a charcoal drawing class at age eight and loving art since then. Dechant attended the University of Wisconsin-Parkside. Daleski attended University of Wisconsin-Parkside and University of Wisconsin-Oshkosh.

Sponsor: Franksville Veterinary Clinic

Catastrophic (for the cat)

"Tables are turned; mice saddle up the cat for the ride of their lives."

Artist: Brooke Wentland, Madison

Brooke Wentland graduated this May from the University of Wisconsin-Madison with a bachelor's degree in fine arts and graphic design concentration. A native of the Green Bay area, her favorite hobby is painting decorative furniture where she turns a plain piece of furniture into a colorful, decorative piece full of character. Other interests include travel, photography, watercolor and athletics.

Sponsor: North Shore Animal Hospital

Don't Ask

"Who knows how this could have happened?"

Artist: Don M. Betts, Racine

Don Betts has been a blacksmith artist since 1957 and a Racine resident since 1968. He has taught industrial arts for 30 years, 22 of them for Racine Unified School District and Gateway Technical College. He enjoys working with metals, both in sculpture and jewelry, though most of his art creations are in iron and steel. He has exhibited in Wisconsin and Illinois.

Sponsor: Dairy Statesmen

One Fish, Two Fish, Cat Fish, Go Fish

"Gone fishing – inside the fish bowl."

Artist: Julie Wynstra, Racine

A lifelong Racine resident, Julie Wynstra attended the University of Wisconsin-Milwaukee. She credits her creativity to her heredity. Wynstra, who works at Gardtec, Inc., is self-taught in the creative arts and enjoys sewing, knitting and crocheting. She once designed a restaurant interior to look like the Flintstone home in Bedrock, and also taught ballet classes and designed the children's costumes.

Sponsor: Gardtec, Inc.

Sparky

"Stay away from electrical cords!"

Artists: The Pond Family, Racine

Sparky is a family project. Gary and Fran Pond are owners of Inter-Med, Inc. (Vista Dental), Racine. Caitlin, a junior at Horlick High School, participates in National Honor Society, Math Club and the varsity tennis team. Nick, in seventh grade at Jerstad Agerholm Middle School, loves to skateboard and is a second-degree black belt in Tae Kwon Do. The Ponds were involved in Dog Days of Summer.

Sponsor: Vista Dental

These six kitty creations show that even the critter known to sleep much of the time can participate successfully in sporting activities.

"If man could be crossed with the cat, it would improve man but would deteriorate the cat."

Mark Twain

Allie the Alley Cat

"Ready for a night at the bowling alley."

Artists: Patti Ontko and Martha Hilgers, Racine

Patti Ontko studied graphic design at Milwaukee Area Technical College and has worked in the printing industry for many years. She is now self-employed and proprietor of Castle Lanes. Martha Hilgers is a seamstress and has been involved in the crafting industry for many years. She currently is an assistant manager and junior bowling coordinator at Castle Lanes.

Sponsor: Castle Lanes

Cat Trick

"A soccer cat just scored his third goal – through the air with a purrfect header."

Artist: Matt Maletis, Racine

Matt Maletis has taught art at Giese Elementary School, Racine, for seven years. He has coached soccer at Washington Park High School for six years. He also coaches the U-14 Racine Soccer Club Fire, the inspiration for his cat. He says the girls have an incredible enthusiasm for learning. He wants to relay that enthusiasm to Cat'n Around Downtown.

Sponsor: WISPARK LLC

Kung Fu Kitty

"In authentic uniform; the head band insignia means 'water.' "

Artist: Reid Pfarr, Kenosha

Reid Pfarr holds a bachelor of arts degree from the University of
Wisconsin-Parkside, where he has taught karate for 27 years. He works on
a wide variety of art continuums, ranging from woodcarving, sculpture
and drawing to restoring classic cars. Pfarr has won numerous awards
for his auto restorations and wood carvings.

Sponsor: Associated Bank

Catty Shack

"Racine golf courses, with the 'catties' hard at work."

Artist: Julie Conigliaro, Racine

A graduate of Cardinal Stritch University in commercial art and
design, Julie Conigliaro is a senior graphic designer at SC Johnson.
An avid athlete, she enjoys bicycling with her hearing dog, Abby, in
tow, as well as golfing, hiking and other sports. Creating and
personalizing her home keeps her busy and she relaxes by playing
her Native American flute.

Sponsor: Sign Pro – Division of Pristine Products

Nascat

"Race cars and checker flags."

Artist: Sheryl A. Meyer, Racine

Currently a pre-school teacher, Sheryl Meyer enjoys using her artistic talent in the education of young children. She likes pencil sketching and working in charcoal. She is a self-taught artist who finds pleasure in painting with acrylics. She has received honors in art contests entered in the United States and Japan and created a canine for last summer's Dog Days of Summer.

Sponsor: Martinizing Dry Cleaning

Pack Cat

"A die-hard Packer fan."

Artist: Evette Sapp-Nasr, Chaska, Minnesota

Evette Sapp-Nasr is a University of Wisconsin-Parkside fine arts graduate. She has participated in various shows and competitions. A Kenosha native now living in Minnesota, she has been and always will be a Green Bay Packer fan. She admires the way some eccentric fans paint their faces. She enjoys painting and drawing in her free time.

Sponsor: Kidd's World Wide Travel

Tail-twitching Transformations

Cats can really be anything they want to be, when they make up their minds to do so. They even assume multiple identities, as shown among these 14 felines.

"Women and cats will do as they please, and men and dogs should relax and get used to the idea."

Robert N. Heinlein

Ain't It a Hoot?

"Is this a cat in owl's clothing?"

Artist: Renee Popadic, Racine

Born and raised in Racine, Renee Popadic has always enjoyed arts and crafts. As an adult, her favorite hobby is working with wood. She has focused her drawing, sculpting and painting talents to create wildlife woodcarvings. Popadic is a member of Racine's Wildlife Carving Club.

Sponsor: CRB Insurance

Calico Catacomb Cat

"Look into the depths of this feline."

Artist: Cecilia E. Smith, Racine

Special education teacher Cecilia Smith works in several media, including watercolor, oil, ink, stained glass, pastels and latex paints. Her work can be seen at Jefferson Lighthouse School in Racine, where she has taught for 12 years, and at the First United Methodist Church on Main Street. She is a graduate of Kansas State University and the University of Wisconsin-Whitewater.

Sponsor: Jefferson Lighthouse Elementary School PTA

Cat-a-log

"This 'punny' pet has gotten into the Linc'n logs."

Artists: Heather Bumstead and Lincoln Friends, Racine

Heather Bumstead is the director of pastoral care at Lincoln Lutheran of Racine. A self-taught artist, she says art is a hobby that feeds the spirit. Pencil sketching and graphic design are her favorite art forms. This year, she had help with her cat from fellow Lincoln staffers. She and a friend also participated in last year's Dog Days of Summer.

Sponsor: Lincoln Lutheran of Racine

"Cat"erpillar

"From caterpillar to cocoon to butterfly."

Artist: Deborah Madigan, West Salem, Ohio

Originally from Racine, Deborah Madigan received her bachelor of fine arts degree from Ohio University and her master's degree in library science from Kent State University. She manages a library for the Wayne County Public Library System in Ohio. A multi-media artist, she works with found objects, paint, collage and drawing materials. Her works have been shown in Arizona, New York and the Midwest.

Sponsor: Triple E Electric Co.

Caterpillar

"From the caterpillar comes the Monarch butterfly."

Artist: Jamie Cassar, Kenosha
A graduate of Alma College in Alma, Michigan, with a bachelor of arts degree in art and design, Jamie Cassar is assistant director of Kenosha's Lemon Street Gallery. The focus of Cassar's artwork revolves around ceramics. Hand-made paper and wire sculpture also interest her. She has taught classes at Charles A. Wustum Museum of Fine Arts and the Kenosha Public Museum.

Sponsor: Molly MaGruder

Caterpillar

"It's the time of year when caterpillars meander along, looking for a place to grow."

Artist: Krista Lea Meinert Edquist, Racine
Shortly after Krista Lea Meinert Edquist received her fine arts degree from the University of Wisconsin-Parkside in 1998, she was commissioned to design the layout for a compact disk project, followed by other work, including a mural for a multi-million-dollar corporation. In 2002 her photographs and sculptures were accepted for Charles A. Wustum Museum of Fine Arts' Tri-County Photographic Print Competition and Racine Area Arts Exhibition.

Sponsor: The Masters of Movement School of the Dance

Caterpillar

"A cat in caterpillar's clothing."

Artist: Sarah Galipeau, Racine

An art teacher at Lance Middle School in Kenosha, Sarah Galipeau graduated from Racine's Washington Park High School. Her degree is from the University of Wisconsin-Parkside, where education was her area of study, with a major in art and an emphasis in sculpture.

Sponsor: A & E Incorporated

Caterpillar

"The metamorphosis of the Monarch, in its natural habitat."

Artist: Angela Perrault, Racine

A lifelong Racine resident, Angela Perrault is a graduate of Horlick High School and holds a bachelor of science degree in nursing from the University of Wisconsin-Milwaukee. Past artistic projects include school play sets, murals for homes and a church, scroll saw woodworking, painting, sewing, watercolors and a calligraphy business. She also enjoys rubber stamping and scrapbooking.

Sponsor: Nielsen Machine Co., Inc.

Dog Days Wanna Be

"This cat has major issues. It wanted to be in last year's Dog Days of Summer."

Artist: Amy E. Carter, Racine

A graduate of the University of Wisconsin-LaCrosse with a bachelor's degree in art, Amy Carter is a graphic designer with SC Johnson. Although her training is in painting and drawing, she enjoys all aspects of digital design. She now loves creating one-of-a-kind art with her two-year-old daughter.

Sponsor: The Samantha Cancer Foundation

Here Kitty, Kitty

"The kitty as an adorable skunk."

Artist: Christopher Sklba, Racine

A Racine native, Christopher Sklba is a graduate of Milwaukee Institute of Art and Design. A professional goldsmith, he has won several Midwest awards for his jewelry designs. Sklba also teaches adult education classes in metals at the Charles A. Wustum Museum of Fine Arts in Racine.

Sponsor: Norco Manufacturing Corporation

Kitty City

"This entire cat makes up its own community."

Artist: Kelly Smith, Racine
A lifelong Racine resident, Kelly Smith has been working in clay since she was in elementary school. She recently has started to display and sell her work. Her first art fair was at the University of Wisconsin-Parkside in 2002. Her works also are available at Funky Hannah's and Lighthouse Framing and Art Gallery, both in Downtown Racine.

Sponsor: Avenue Frame Shop and Gallery

Octopus

"This magnificent creature is the envy of all the cat world."

Artist: Krista Lea Meinert Edquist, Racine
Shortly after Krista Lea Meinert Edquist received her fine arts degree from the University of Wisconsin-Parkside in 1998, she was commissioned to design the layout for a compact disk project, followed by other work, including a mural for a multi-million-dollar corporation. In 2002 her photographs and sculptures were accepted for Charles A. Wustum Museum of Fine Arts' Tri-County Photographic Print Competition and Racine Area Arts Exhibition.

Sponsor: Sustainable Racine

Pussywillow

"This cat wears the 18th century Willow Ware dinnerware pattern."

Artist: Jamie Cassar, Kenosha

A graduate of Alma College in Alma, Michigan, with a bachelor of arts degree in art and design, Jamie Cassar is assistant director of Kenosha's Lemon Street Gallery. The focus of Cassar's artwork revolves around ceramics. Hand-made paper and wire sculpture also interest her. She has taught classes at Charles A. Wustum Museum of Fine Arts and the Kenosha Public Museum.

Sponsor: Beauty Unlimited Inc.

The Whole Kit and Cat-Poodle

"A sewing kitty – or is it really a dog?"

Artist: Kevin Pearson, Franksville

Kevin Pearson grew up in Moline, Illinois, and graduated from Augustana College. After an apprenticeship in clay, he operated a pottery studio in Egg Harbor, Wisconsin, for 10 years. Pearson has been at The Prairie School in Racine for the past 24 years as a teacher or administrator. He currently is the head of the art department.

Sponsor: Beth Tagtmeier

The Honored Cats

Cleocatra

Catfish

Cat Fishing in Winter

"The cats are fantastic! They are creative, original, humorous, colorful, conceptual. Wow!"

So said Janet Tenneson-McCarty of Mequon, who in early May judged the 151 cats in Downtown Racine's Cat'n Around Downtown, determining which cats would receive the $3,000, $2,000 and $1,000 prizes awarded by Downtown Racine Corporation. Winners were announced in June.

"The diversity of media used – paint, wood, metal, mosaic, fabric, ceramic, and more – and the skill in execution of the cat concepts are remarkable," she added.

Tenneson-McCarty has been an artist for many years and holds masters of arts degrees from Marquette University in English literature and the University of Wisconsin-Oshkosh in art. She also studied at Vermont Studio Center with Wolf

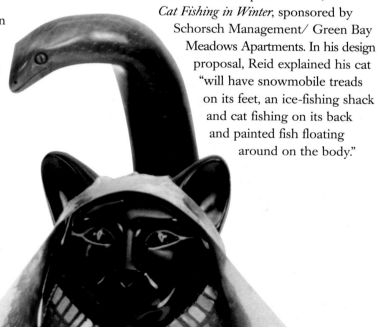

Kahn and Katherine Porter. Her work has been exhibited at galleries throughout Wisconsin and is found in corporate, public and private collections nationwide. She has received many awards at both the state and national levels.

She spent 14 years as a corporate art consultant, judging and selecting art to be used in public spaces nationwide. She now devotes her time to her own studio work and exhibitions in several galleries. Her works currently are on exhibit at Edgewood Orchard Galleries in Fish Creek, Wisconsin; Art Elements in Mequon; Katie Gingrass Gallery in Milwaukee; and Lake Country Gallery in Pewaukee, Wisconsin and Naples, Florida.

"Creativity of this quality will add to the spirit and quality of life in the Downtown Racine area," Tenneson-McCarty said. "The artistic cats are an inspiration and a tribute to the Racine community.

"I am excited about my plans to come to Racine with friends to see the cats installed in their public places," she added.

Top Honors

First place winner is *Catfish*, created by Denise Roberts McKee of Racine and sponsored by Stunt Puppy Entertainment, Inc. In her design proposal, McKee explained that her cat "will be a mosaic piece created from pieces of colored tile and smooth glass. The sculpture will consist of a series of brightly colored fish designs surrounded by a light blue 'ocean' background. The overall color scheme is tropical in nature: yellows, reds, blues, purples and greens."

Cleocatra, created by Janet Mrazek of Racine, David Gaura of Franksville and Linda Morafcik of Kenosha, and sponsored by Aurora Health Care, received second place honors. In the design proposal, the artists said "this cat will portray the beauty and majesty of Cleopatra in her fine headdress and beautiful snake jewelry. She'll even wear tiny sandals."

Bill Reid of Racine created the third place winner, *Cat Fishing in Winter*, sponsored by Schorsch Management/ Green Bay Meadows Apartments. In his design proposal, Reid explained his cat "will have snowmobile treads on its feet, an ice-fishing shack and cat fishing on its back and painted fish floating around on the body."

High Honors

Tenneson-McCarty awarded high honors to the following:

ACAT, created by Bruce Renquist,
sponsored by Dover Flag and Map.

A Cat's House, created by Marcia Sykes,
sponsored by Re/Max Southwest, Inc.

Ain't It a Hoot?, created by Renee Popadic,
sponsored by CRB Insurance.

Ar-cat-ecture, created by Julia Fawcett,
sponsored by Bluelines, Inc.

Belle's Root River Holiday, created by Linda Silvasi-Kelly,
sponsored by Harbor Lite Yacht Club.

Bobcat, created by Don Bugalecki,
sponsored by Johnson Outdoors.

Cat 'n Hats, created by Sybil Brauneis Klug,
sponsored by Nordik of America.

Caterpillar, created by Krista Lea Meinert Edquist,
sponsored by The Masters of Movement School of Dance.

Kittyhawk, created by Candace Walters,
sponsored by Design Partners, Inc.

Right Up My Alley, created by Julie Trafton,
sponsored by Britten Road Press.

Honorable Mention

The following cats received honorable mentions:

Artistocat, created by Debra DeKeuster and Meeka Droese,
sponsored by Lutheran High School Booster Club.

Cat-"Tails", created by Sue Horton,
sponsored by the Horton Family.

Cat Gut, created by Barbara Lingquist,
sponsored by Olympia Brown Unitarian Universalist
Women's Federation.

Cat with a "Mousey" Brown Coat, created by Carla Marie Reed,
sponsored by W. H. Pugh.

CATerpillar, created by Angela Perrault,
sponsored by Nielsen Machine Co., Inc.

Cat's Delights, created by Kristin Gjerdset,
sponsored by Educators Credit Union.

Cleocatra and the Kitten Kingdom, created by Karen Johnston,
sponsored by *The Journal Times*.

Cop 'n Kiddies, created by Sr. Janet Weyker,
sponsored by Quota International of Kenosha-Racine.

Copy Cat, created by J. S. Adams,
sponsored by Robert W. Baird.

Don't Ask, created by Don M. Betts,
sponsored by Dairy Statesmen.

Ho (B) Kat, created by Peg Ducommun,
sponsored by Myrna Pat Bellomy.

Kitty City, created by Kelly Smith,
sponsored by Avenue Frame Shop and Gallery.

Louis Quatorze, created by Flo Walker,
sponsored by Landmark Title of Racine, Inc.

Meowscles, created by Jeff Levonian,
sponsored by Dimple's Fine Imports.

NASCAT, created by Sheryl A. Meyer,
sponsored by Martinizing Dry Cleaning.

One Fish Two Fish Cat Fish Go Fish,
created by Julie Wynstra, sponsored by Gardtec, Inc.

Pussywillow, created by Jamie Cassar,
sponsored by Beauty Unlimited Inc.

Sourpuss, created by Teresa Meyers,
sponsored by Porters of Racine.

Tabbey Road, created by Paul Muckler,
sponsored by Adecco Technical.

The Cheshire Cat, created by Melanie Pope,
sponsored by Racine Public Library.

When the Cat's a Whey the Mice Will Play,
created by Amy Zahalka,
sponsored by Friends of Racine
Heritage Museum.

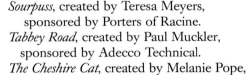

Mission Statement:

The Downtown Racine Corporation will be the leader in the continued economic, aesthetic and recreational revitalization of Downtown and its neighborhoods.

We will be proactive in the retention of existing business. We will facilitate new developments by promoting public/private investments and partnerships, and working cooperatively with the other economic development organizations.

In all that we do, we will communicate effectively with our members, partners, many diversified neighbors and the public at large.

Vision Statement:

Downtown Racine will be:
- A symbol of the community's pride.
- A center of celebration and recreation on the lake.
- A harmonious mixture of residential, commercial, cultural, recreational and governmental activities.
- A safe, convenient and aesthetically pleasing place to live, work, shop, visit and play.
- Respectful of its historical character, its charm and waterfront setting.
- Pedestrian and driver-friendly with efficient traffic circulation, signage and convenient and safe parking.
- A unique retail center serving the needs of its neighborhood, the community and visitors.
- People-oriented and neighborhood for all neighbors.

Board of Directors:

Chairman: Brian Anderson, SC Johnson
Vice Chairman: Micah Waters, Porters of Racine
Secretary: Fiona Zaleski, Community Volunteer
Treasurer: Scott Kelly, Johnson Bank

Government Officials:

Gary Becker, Mayor
William McReynolds, County Executive
Cherri Cape, Alderman

Board:

Lynne Ciaramita, Lakeview Pharmacy
John Crimmings, N. Christensen and Son Real Estate, Inc.
Dave Foster, Design Partners, Inc.
Jerry Franke, WISPARK LLC
Brad Harring, Avenue Frame Shop and Gallery
Jane Hutterly, SC Johnson
Dick Johnston, The Journal Times
Joanne Labre, Dover Flag
Mary Beth Ormiston, Racine Family YMCA
Bernard Powers, Knuteson, Wheeler and Powers, S.C.
Jim Spodick, Historic Century Market
Mike Staeck, Landmark Title

Downtown Racine Corporation Staff:

Kathy Hansen, Executive Director
Lennie Farrington, Receptionist
Jean Garbo, Marketing Director
Terry Leopold, Special Events Coordinator
Elaina McLain, Accountant
Laurie Pettit, Marketing Assistant

An architectural rendering shows Downtown Racine Corporation's vision of a renovated Main Street in Downtown Racine.

Index of Artist Profiles

118

Index of Cat Portraits

119

Index of Sponsors